WILD DINGO

Leesa Smith

Illustrations by Sophie Taylor

Published by Boolarong Press in collaboration with Goanna Tales publishing.
38/1631 Wynnum Road
Tingalpa Qld 4173, Australia.
www.boolarongpress.com.au

First published 2026

ISBN: 9781923321137 (paperback)

Printed and bound by Watson & Ferguson Company, Tingalpa, Australia

A catalogue record for this book is available from the National Library of Australia

This Goanna Tales book belongs to:

____

Dingo roams down to the edge of the sea,
nose near the sand sniffing tidal debris.

He trots down the beach leaving tracks in the sand,
and patiently waits where the fishermen stand.

Dingo knows too well the fishermen's game,
keen ocean hunters, their goal is the same.

He watches taut lines pull fresh fish from the sea,
lured by the thrill of a meal caught for free.

A swish of a tail, silver flash of the catch,
dares dingo closer, jaws ready to snatch...

...a snippet of tail, head, fin or gleaned bone,
the fisherman mindlessly to him has thrown.

Day fades, light lingers, it's late afternoon,
dingo sits high, ancient King of the dunes.

Close by kids paddle, they play, chase and scamp,
as sun-soaked families head back to their camp.

Cars trail sand tracks up and under the trees,
where wide open tents catch the cool misty breeze.

Dingo roams close. Scents of food waft about.
He nips at a child in his way, people shout!

Dingo stands strong, hackles line up his back.
A child turns to run, dingo's on the attack.

Men yell, sticks raised. Women scoop kids up high.
'Get rid of wild dogs, keep us safe,' they all cry!

BEWARE
WILD DINGOS

*Rangers close in, tracking dogs with no fear.
Protection? Or our loss? The confusion is clear.*

News stories tell us wild dogs are to blame,
but these aren't our pets, we can't treat them the same.

NEWS TODAY
TRACKERS ARE
NHILL TIMES
AR JOURNAL
NOTHER ATTACK

ESKY

Dingoes learn quickly where food can be found,
so give them no reason to linger around.

Wildlife surrounds us, watch how they behave.
Respect where they live, and don't stand in their way.

Our freedom is something so precious we share,
to stay your distance simply shows that you care.

The Dingo is Australia's wild dog.
They are not like a pet dog.

They are hunters, living alone, or in groups. They communicate with other dingoes by howling, not barking.

Dingoes live in many areas of Australia.

National Park Rangers say –

Never feed or approach dingoes.

Keep a good distance from dingoes.

Stay together. Walk in a group and carry a stick.

Calmly back away when they are near. Never run.

Store food and rubbish securely.

GLOSSARY

Tidal – *the ocean's water levels rising and falling*

Debris – *scattered pieces of something left on the beach*

Taut – *stretched very tight*

Lured – *to tempt something closer*

Linger – *to stay longer than necessary*

Ancient – *very, very old*

Waft – *a scent, carried through the air by a gentle breeze*

Hackles – *hairs on a dingo's neck and back that stand up when it's scared or angry*

Precious – *something very special, valuable, or important.*

AUTHOR BIO:

Leesa Smith is a teacher, author and publisher based in Queensland. Her love of the outdoors and camping adventures with her family, provides inspiration for her stories. When writing, Leesa integrates shared elements of our rich Australian culture and glimpses of our contrasting environments, within her story texts and illustrations. Her purpose in writing and publishing children's literature is to produce quality Australian reading resources which can be of use both at home and at school.

ARTIST BIO:

Sophie Taylor is a Gamilaraay artist and mother, working as a creative director, costume designer, performer, ceramicist and illustrator. With over ten years of experience as a practicing artist and cultural workshop facilitator, Sophie has dedicated her career to celebrating Indigenous culture. She studied Contemporary Australian Indigenous Art at the Queensland College of Art (QCA) and currently works for a local Indigenous non-profit organisation, supporting her community through cultural programs.